Verses Of Love And Transformation

Luna Mhelle Grace

Made with ❤ on the BookLeaf Publishing Platform
www.bookleafpub.in
www.bookleafpub.com

Dedication

To the resilient souls who find beauty in their scars, and to the dreamers who believe in the power of love to heal and transform. This collection is for you, who have walked through the storms and emerged stronger, who have embraced both the light and the shadows within. And to myself, as I continue on my journey of transformation, discovering new depths of strength and love within. May these poems be a mirror to our journeys, a beacon of hope, and a celebration of the incredible transformations that unfold within us.

With love and gratitude, this book is dedicated to our courage, our growth, and our unwavering hearts.

Preface

Life is a journey filled with moments of profound love and transformation. In those moments, we find ourselves growing, healing, and discovering new facets of our true selves. This collection of poems is a heartfelt testament to those experiences—a celebration of love in its many forms and a reflection of the transformative power it holds.

As you immerse yourself in these verses, I hope you feel the connection to your own journey. These poems are born from my heart, capturing the essence of self-love, the beauty of self-discovery, and the strength found in personal growth and empowerment. They are an invitation to you—to embrace your own path, to find solace in your own experiences, and to recognize the courage and resilience within you.

This book is a companion on your journey, offering words of comfort, inspiration, and understanding. Whether you are navigating through pain, joy, healing, or transformation, may you find a piece of your own story within these pages. May these poems remind you that you are not alone and that every step you take towards self-love and growth is a testament to your incredible strength.

Thank you for joining me on this poetic voyage. Here's to the love that heals, the growth that empowers, and the journey that transforms us all.

With gratitude and hope,
Luna Mhelle Grace

Acknowledgements

This book is a labor of love, and it wouldn't have come to life without the unwavering support of many wonderful people. First and foremost, I am deeply grateful to my family and friends. Your unconditional love and encouragement have been my anchors, giving me the strength and inspiration to pour my heart into these poems. Thank you for believing in me, even when I doubt myself.

To my readers, thank you for embarking on this journey with me. Your willingness to open your hearts to these words means more than you can imagine. I hope these poems resonate with your experiences and offer you comfort, hope, and empowerment. You are not alone on this path.

A special thank you to my editor, whose thoughtful feedback and meticulous attention to detail have shaped this collection into what it is today. Your dedication to this craft is truly appreciated.

To the community of poets and writers, thank you for your creativity and for reminding me of the power of words. Your work has been a constant source of inspiration and motivation.

Lastly, I want to acknowledge my own journey. This book is a reflection of my experiences, the highs and lows, the moments of joy and pain. Through this process, I have learned the transformative power of love and self-discovery. I am grateful for every step along the way.

With deep appreciation and heartfelt gratitude,
Luna Mhelle Grace

Me, Myself, and I

In the quiet of the me, a whisper soft and clear,
A journey of a thousand steps, begins with self so near.
Through the lens of introspection, thoughts freely fly,
I embark upon this voyage, with me, myself, and I.

Myself, the heart's own mirror, reflecting inner truth,
A tapestry of memories, the old entwined with youth.
With every beat, a story, a dream beneath the sky,
I weave a tale of passion, with me, myself, and I.

And I, the soul's bold traveler, paths both wide and tight,
Embracing every moment, from morning to night.
With open arms, I venture, where hopes and dreams ally,
I seek to share my essence, with me, myself, and I.

This series of existences, a trilogy of grace,
A dance of deep connection, in life's expansive space.
To touch the hearts of others, to laugh, to love, to cry,
Is to live a life worth living, with me, myself, and I.

Me Against the World

I live half a lifetime, trying to fit in a matrix
That the world shapes for me, yet never feels like home.
I follow all the rules, trying to be a good person
But I feel like a fool, pretending to be someone else.

I sacrifice my dreams, trying to please everyone else
But I always feel like a scream, trapped in a silent shell.
Now I'm in mid-life, and I wonder what it's all for
Do I have to live in strife, or choose something more?

I want to discover who I am, beyond the expectations
I want to embrace my plan and find my true passions.
I want to break free, away from the cage built for me
I want to turn a new page and write my own story.

I know it won't be easy, facing doubts and fears
But I also know it's worth it, living the rest of my years.
I'm not too late to start, not too weak to challenge
I'm ready to find myself, defy what the world dictates.

Echoes of Self-Worth

In the shadows of my doubts, I wander lost and small,
A mirror reflecting flaws, a heart that seems to fall.
The world spins on its axis, yet I stand still, unsure,
Seeking solace in echoes of my own whispered allure.

I wear masks like armor, veil my fragile core,
Chasing validation, seeking worth beyond the door.
But deep within the tempest, the truth begins to stir,
Self-worth blooms within, not from what others confer.

The battle rage within me, a tempest fierce and wild,
A personal crisis, a soul adrift, yearning for a smile.
But I vow to find my compass, to chart a course anew,
I embrace the broken pieces, weaving something true.

I strip away the layers, the expectations and the lies,
Unravel the knots of self-doubt, let vulnerability rise.
In the void of my brokenness, I glimpse a hidden light,
A mosaic of resilience, waiting to take flight.

I whisper and say, "You are more than what you see,
Not define by judgments or the weight of history."
And as the storm subsided, a revelation unfurls,
Self-worth blooms within, in rawness of my world.

Dancing with vulnerability, hands with my scars,
Finding strength in imperfections, tracing the stars.
Self-worth isn't a destination, but a journey I grasp,
A symphony of self-love, a canvas where grace alight.

Here's to broken moments, a phoenix rising from ash,
Finding self-worth in scars, in vulnerability's clash.
Within my reflection, is the universe's song,
For in crisis, I discover that I am worthy all along.

The Warrior Within

In harsh whispers, my critic speaks,
Through shadows cast, my spirit seeks,
To drown in doubts, to fear the flaws,
Yet strength within me claws and claws.

The mirror shows a face unseen,
A blend of both the kind and mean,
But past the cracks, a warrior stands,
To fight the thoughts with steadfast hands.

The voice inside, so quick to judge,
Yet love and truth refuse to budge,
For deep within, I'm worth the praise,
Through darkest nights and brightest days.

Each step I take, though filled with worry,
Becomes a tale, an epic story,
Of battles won against my fears,
Of triumphs told through whispered cheers.

With every scar, a lesson learned,
With every doubt, a fire burned,
My heart grows strong, my mind set free,
To be the best that I can be.

In moments dark, when hope seems lost,
I remember this, at any cost,
The critic's voice is just a part,
But not the whole, within my heart.

So, I rise above self-disdain,
Embracing myself, through joy and pain,
For I am more than voices say,
A bright beacon, to light the way.

From Shadows to Sunshine

In cast shadows, my past revealed,
With harsh whispers, my wounds unsealed,
Yet deep within, I find the fire,
To face the dark and climb the spire.

The burdens borne, my heart weighed down,
Mistakes that tried to steal my crown,
But through the pain, I see the grace,
That lessons learned, the soul's embrace.

Each misstep taken is a chance to soar,
A clearer view, I've never had before,
I let regrets and sorrow fade,
To find the strength within me laid.

The past is a tale that's etched in time,
Yet here I stand with thoughts sublime,
With hope renewed and vast courage,
I break the chains, free at last.

Self-forgiveness is a steep journey,
With every scar, a deep story,
The guilt I shed, the past I free,
To be the best that I can be.

In every breath, a spark of change,
In every step, a new range,
I hold no grudge against my past,
For it has shaped my strength at last.

So here I stand with an open heart,
Embracing now, a brand-new start,
The past behind, the future bright,
I walk with hope into the light.

Free from Conformity

In my childhood days, my heart was wild and free,
A canvas of dreams, unbound, untouched by fear.
Imagination soared on wings so pure,
A world of wonders, each moment is a treasure.

No boundaries held my mind's vast expanse,
Each thought and idea danced without restraint.
The world was mine, a playground so vast,
No whispers of doubt, no shadows faint.

But as I grew, the world imposed its mold,
Expectations whispered, loud and cold.
Conformity's chains wrapped 'round my soul,
Demanding I fit within its narrow role.

Who am I, in this complex masquerade?
A mirror's reflection, or a mask well-played?
Identity shifts, like sand through hands,
Caught between who I am and who life demands.

Stereotypes paint walls around my core,
A fractured self, torn and unsure.
The quest for self, a labyrinthine plight,
Through shifting shadows, seeking the light.

I long for days when hearts were fearless and bold,
When identity was crafted by my hands.
A yearning for freedom lost in time's cruel fold,
To break the chains and reclaim life's grand plans.

For in the heart's deep core, a truth remains,
That freedom's fire can never be fully tamed.
A journey to rediscover self's pure strains,
In defiance of society's rigid claims.

In search of self, through life's tangled maze,
I seek the light to illuminate the haze.
To find the me, beneath the masks I wear,
And live authentically, with courage and care.

Beyond the Mirror

In a world where looks define the gold,
Where standards are sharp and harsh take hold,
I tread a path both known and strange,
Seeking confidence through this exchange.

The mirror's glance feels harsh and cold,
A tale of flaws both known and bold,
Insecurities whisper coarse,
Their shadows cast deep-rooted fear.

Voices loud and standards clear,
Mold the way I should appear,
Inside, a plea to just be me,
To break these chains, to set me free.

Body image, a cruel guise,
Affects my worth in many eyes,
Opportunities slip and fade,
With confidence oftentimes betrayed.

Yet through the fog, I see the light,
My realization is taking flight,
With true character, a gem so rare,
Outshines the looks, beyond compare.

With every stride, I seek to find,
A sense of peace, a free mind,
Embracing all that's truly me,
And letting go of what should be.

So here I stand, in proud defiance,
Breaking free and budding alliance,
With grace and strength, I rise anew,
Embracing self, with confidence so true.

Balancing Joy with Duty

Amid the tasks that fill my day,
The grind of life, the bills to pay,
I seek a spark, a flame so bright,
To bring back joy, to reignite.

In quiet moments, I explore so deep,
The hidden joys, I can't reject,
Words that echo heartbeat, a tune so sweet,
New hobbies found, makes a life complete.

The chores still call, the duties nigh,
Yet in between, I reach for the sky,
A book to read, a plant to grow,
In simple acts, I start to glow.

The weight of life can press so hard,
Responsibilities caught off guard,
But in these moments, small and true,
I find my heart, my soul anew.

With every joy I choose to seek,
A life of passion, not so meek,
I weave in fun, amidst the stress,
A blend of work and pure finesse.

So now I stand with renewed mind,
In every hobby, moments find,
I balance both joy and strife,
A dancing act to my vibrant life.

Reclaiming My Power

In love's embrace, I'd lose my way,
Let others lead, both night and day,
In tangled webs of others' strife,
Forgot my own, my weary life.

Each call for help, I answered fast,
To be their anchor, steady, vast,
Yet in their storms, my soul was drained,
Their burdens on my shoulders chained.

It felt so right, to be their shield,
In every wound, my heart appealed,
Yet slowly, strength would slip away,
Their struggles left my spirit gray.

At last, I learned to draw a line,
To place a guard, both firm and fine,
A boundary born of self-respect,
A heart once lost, I must protect.

With courage found, I voiced my needs,
In quiet acts and gentle deeds,
For love that's pure will understand,
Boundaries built, with resolute hand.

No longer lost in others' plight,
I found my path, my inner light,
A balanced life, both strong and free,
A love that flows, resiliently.

So now I stand, with my heart aligned,
Embracing self, in peace of mind,
No longer weighed by others' woes,
In every step, my true self shows.

Light Amidst Shadows

In deep shadows, my mind does dwell,
With anxious thoughts that cast a spell,
The future looms, a vast unknown,
Yet seeds of hope, within are sown.

The present brings its weight and strife,
A constant churn, the wheel of life,
Yet in each moment, joy can bloom,
A fleeting light amidst the gloom.

Disappointment holds the past so tight,
It grips like iron, steals my light,
Yet through acceptance, I can find,
A path to free my troubled mind.

Meaning's quest, a lifelong chase,
In every heartbeat, it finds its place,
Through love, through dreams, through simple cheer,
The compass points to what are so dear.

With courage drawn from deep within,
I face the storm, the doubts that spin,
For purpose found is worth the fight,
A guiding star, to a beacon bright.

So here I stand, with my heart aligned,
Embracing life, its ties that bind,
With strength, with grace, I pave my way,
And find my peace in every day.

A Dawn of Love

In your eyes, I find my dawn,
A light so pure, it's never gone.
Each word you speak, my heart ignites,
A dance of souls, in tender flights.

Your touch is a spark, so gentle and true,
It weaves a world for just us two.
We walk on paths of dreams and stars,
Hand in hand, erasing scars.

The past dissolves, like morning mist,
In your embrace, our souls have kissed.
Together, we are whole and free,
A love reborn, just you and me.

With every breath, our hearts align,
A symphony, both yours and mine.
The future shines, a golden hue,
In this moment, love feels new.

We build a world, our hearts in sync,
On hopes and dreams, we dare to think.
Through every trial, strong we'll stand,
United by our love's command.

In your eyes, I see my dawn,
A love that's true, forever drawn.
Together, we'll embrace the light,
A new beginning, shining so bright.

Hearts Across Horizons

Miles apart, yet hearts entwined,
Our love, a bond so rare to find.
Each day we share a sweet embrace,
Across the distance, we find grace.

I wake to whispers through the phone,
Your voice, my solace, when alone.
In dreams, I feel your warm caress,
A love so strong, it knows no less.

Though oceans vast and mountains high,
Our hearts still meet beneath the sky.
With every letter, call, and sigh,
We bridge the gap, you and I.

I trace your words with gentle hands,
A love that grows in foreign lands.
Each moment spent, a treasure dear,
In longing, we find comfort here.

The nights are long, but hope persists,
In every star, your presence kissed.
Our future bright, a distant shore,
Where we will meet and part no more.

Miles apart, yet hearts entwined,
Our love, a truth that's undefined.
With every beat, our souls align,
In this distance, love does shine.

Timeless Connection

In shadows past, my heart has roamed,
Through echoes of love, never fully owned.
With weary steps, I seek a light,
A soul to end this endless night.

Each tear, a whisper of lost dreams,
In every heartache, silent screams.
I yearn for one who sees me true,
In their embrace, to start anew.

A soulmate's touch, a guiding hand,
To lift me up, to help me stand.
Through every storm, and darkest hour,
Together strong, a love to flower.

The nights grow cold, yet hope remains,
A spark of love through all the pains.
In every prayer, my heart does plea,
For one whose love will set me free.

No more the scars of broken ties,
With each goodbye, a heart that cries.
I dream of love that lasts through time,
A soulmate's song, a perfect rhyme.

In shadows past, my heart has roamed,
But now I seek a love that's honed.
With open arms, my soul's request,
To find the one, my heart's true quest.

Love in Shadows

In every smile, I hide my pain,
A love so deep, yet all in vain.
I give my heart, my soul, my all,
But in your eyes, I feel so small.

I bend and break to see you smile,
Each sacrifice, a lonely mile.
Your joy, my beacon, guiding light,
Yet in your shadow, I lose sight.

I hold you close, through every storm,
My love for you, a constant norm.
But in your heart, a distant space,
No warmth returned, no soft embrace.

I pour my soul into your hands,
Yet emptiness is all that stands.
Your happiness, my endless quest,
While my own heart is put to rest.

I wonder why I still hold on,
To dreams and hopes that now feel gone.
A love unreturned, a silent cry,
In deep shadows, I say goodbye.

In every smile, I hide my pain,
A love so deep, yet all in vain.
I'll find my strength, my heart reclaims,
And in the end, I'll heal my name.

Duality of Devotion

In the quiet of my mind, two voices intertwine,
Love for you is so pure, yet logic draws the line.
Mind whispers sternly, urging me to see,
The careful path of reason, where I should let you be.

Yet my heart beats wildly, passion's fervent plea,
In your love I find solace, where I'm meant to be.
Mind crafts boundaries, seasoned by the years,
Heart leaps over walls, undaunted by my fears.

Logic paints a canvas, with certainty and grace,
A future well-defined, avoiding love's embrace.
But my heart's vivid palette, splashes hues unseen,
In the dreams it weaves, love reigns as the queen.

I stand at the crossroads, where paths diverge and sway,
One marked by clear reason, the other by the sway.
Heart's whisper grow louder, a symphony so bright,
While logic holds a lantern, illuminating night.

Each beat, each breath, a testament to this strife,
Caught in love's embrace, the dance of life.
Mind's firm embrace, heart's longing for the thrill,
Which path to follow, which destiny to fulfill?

In this delicate balance, I find myself anew,
Bound by love for you, with a heart so true.
Perhaps the answer lies in the blend of two,
A harmony of reason, and love's eternal view.

Embracing the Unknown

In shadows cast by future's unknown face,
I walk with my heart unsure, a timid pace.
The fear of steps that lead to realms unshown,
Can shake my soul, but courage stands alone.

Judgment's eyes, the critics' cutting voice,
A choir of doubt that leaves me little choice.
Yet still I rise, with strength I find inside,
For true self-worth, in judgment, does not hide.

Failure looms, a ghost outside my door,
A cloak of loss that makes me fear what's more.
But when I fall, I learn, I grow, I see,
A lesson found, a seed of strength in me.

With every dawn, the future's page is bare,
My fears dissolve as dreams begin to dare.
Embrace the night, the dark is but a phase,
For stars will shine, their light a silent praise.

Rejection's sting, a hurt that bleeds within,
Yet scars remind me of the fights I win.
In hopeful heart, I find my ground to stand,
To love myself, a fortress strong and grand.

So I conquer fear, let faith and hope be near,
For life's true journey starts when doubts are clear.
With an open heart, embrace what lies ahead,
A tale of courage in the path I tread.

Rising Strong

When shadows fall and darkness wraps me tight,
I find the strength within to stand and fight.
The weight of failures passes upon my chest,
I rise again, determined, never rest.
For every stumble, every tear I shed,
I learn to walk on paths that lie ahead.

In moments when despair consumes my mind,
I search for rays of hope I know I'll find.
Life's challenges, like mountains tall and grand,
I climb with faith, each step a firm demand.
Through valleys deep and storms that test my will,
I persevere, my heart and soul are still.

When dreams are shattered, scattered by the breeze,
I gather the fragments, mending with such ease.
Though setbacks try to hold me in their grasp,
I break their chains with one determined clasp.
Resilience grows within a mighty tree,
Its roots in strength, its branches reaching free.

In times of doubt, when confidence is thin,
I look within and feel the fire begin.
A spark ignites, a flame of courage so bright,
To face the fears and conquer them with might.
For every setback, every fall I face,
I rise anew, with dignity and grace.

Through trials tough and moments of despair,
I find my way with faith beyond compare.
The road is rough, the journey long and wide,
But I'm not swayed, for strength is on my side.
With every challenge, every hurdle crossed,
I find new strength in all that I've embossed.

So here I stand, unbroken by the past,
A testament to strength that's built to last.
Through every storm and every heavy rain,
I rise once more, embracing all the pain.
For setbacks are but steps along the way,
To greater heights and brighter, hopeful days.

Gratitude's Embrace

In the quiet morning light, I find my heart still whole,
Setbacks lay before me, like shadows on my soul.
Yet amidst the trials, I uncover hidden grace,
In every small blessing, I see a smiling face.

I breathe in the air, let go of past despair,
Gratitude blooms softly, weaving through my care.
Each challenge I encounter, a lesson in disguise,
A chance to see the world through grateful, wiser eyes.

I gather strength within, from moments I've endured,
Grateful for resilience, by hardships reassured.
The sun may hide behind the clouds, the rain may fall,
But in the storm's embrace, I find moments to seize.

Each step I take is mindful, each breath a song of thanks,
For in my heart, I carry treasures, filling up the blanks.
Setbacks may try to shake me, but gratitude prevails,
Anchoring my spirit, like ships against the gales.

I hold on to the present, the gift of here and now,
Appreciating every day, and to this life I vow.
To cultivate a mindset, where gratitude will reign,
In setbacks, I find beauty, in the heart's enduring flame.

My Place, My Voice

In a world where echoes of the past still sway,
I find my voice determined to convey.
With courage in my heart, I step to claim,
A place where strength and spirit fan the flame.

In rooms where whispers try to silence me,
I speak with clarity, my truth runs free.
For every doubt, a louder truth I share,
To carve my space with words beyond compare.

Though barriers stand tall, I rise above,
With every challenge met with strength and love.
I break the chains that seek to bind my will,
My voice unwavering, my heart is still.

In moments when the world attempts to hide,
I stand with pride and never step aside.
For in my soul, a boundless power lies,
To challenge norms and reach up to the skies.

With every step, I find my rightful place,
A tapestry of strength, adorned with grace.
For in this world, I forge my path anew,
A woman's voice, both fierce and true.

And so I walk, with purpose in each stride,
My voice, my place, where dreams and strength collide.
In this domain, once ruled by others' might,
I shine as beacon in the darkest night.

Unyielding Grace

I stand with strength, unwavering and bold,
Within my heart, a fire never cold.
In face of storms, I rise with steady grace,
A beacon shining bright in every place.

Through trials faced, my spirit never breaks,
With each new challenge, deeper roots I take.
My courage blooms like flowers in the spring,
A testament to all the strength I bring.

When darkness falls, I light the path ahead,
My will unyielding, even when I dread.
I find the power within my very soul,
To rise again and reach my highest goal.

With empathy, I weave my love and care,
A gentle touch that heals and yet is rare.
For strength is found in kindness and in love,
In every act, a testament thereof.

Through whispered doubts and times of sheer despair,
I hold my ground, embracing every prayer.
For in my heart, a fierce resolve resides,
A strength that through the storm, forever guides.

So here I stand, a woman strong and free,
Embracing all that life may bring to me.
With every step, my true essence unfolds,
A story of strength, and courage untold.

Seeds of Purpose

I forgive the shadows of my past,
Lessons learned, they shape my soul,
With each misstep, my heart's steadfast,
In life's grand dance, I find my course.

I discover passions, fiery and bright,
They ignite my soul, my guiding light,
In love and dreams, I find delight,
Building bonds that feel just right.

Within, I unearth my true essence,
Listening to my heart's gentle song,
Embracing desires, where dreams begin,
My purpose unfolds where I belong.

Acts of service, my heart extends,
In kindness shared, my soul finds peace,
Through helping others, my journey bends and weaves,
In love's embrace, my doubts are released.

With open arms, I embrace the day,
Forgiving the shadows that once held tight,
Through passion's flame, I see the light,
Through the light of love, embracing life.

Connection grows with grace bestowed,
Kind words and deeds, my sacred space,
A life of meaning, built on love and understanding,
In serving others, a legacy of tender grace.

Here I stand, with purpose so bright,
Embraced by life, my soul's delight,
In love's true light, my heart feels free,
I find my true self, in love and light.